FOLKESTONE THEN AND NOW

ALL IN COLOUR

By Nicholas Reed

Folkestone Harbour, probably in the 1960s

PUBLISHED BY
Lilburne Press
7 Wingate Road
Folkestone, Kent
CT19 5QE
Tel: 01303 257 659
Email lilburnepress@hotmail.com
www.lilburnepress.co.uk

ISBN 978 1 901167 17 7

This edition published in Great Britain in 2007 by

PUBLISHED BY
Lilburne Press
7 Wingate Road
Folkestone, Kent
CT19 5QE
Tel: 01303 257 659
Email: lil   Email   l.com
Website: lilburnepress@hotmail.com   co.uk
www.lilburnepress.co.uk

ISBN 978 1 90116717 7

FOLKESTONE THEN AND NOW
ALL IN COLOUR
By Nicholas Reed

Introduction

The sea front at Folkestone is likely to change its appearance dramatically in the next few years. The establishment of The Creative Foundation and the intended development of a new Arts University will be major contributors to these changes, all thanks to the far-sighted generosity of Roger de Haan, the former owner of Saga.

This book is partly to remind us of how the town appeared when it was more "spacious and gracious" than it is now. But it may also serve as a useful record of its appearance along the coast at the start of the 21st century.

The Use of Colour

As far as I know, this is the first time a local history book has used colour when putting together photographs of Then and Now. Normally, both old and modern photos are reproduced in black and white. Occasionally, one will find a modern colour photo showing the view now, but old black and white photos used to illustrate the past. But once the scenes from the past are also in colour, not only is comparison made easier, but the earlier scenes seem much more vivid.

How to Use this book

This book is arranged, and can be followed, as a series of three walks around Folkestone. For those walking, the interest may be in seeing changes since the modern photos were taken.

The first walk starts at the Harbour, takes one east to the Sunny Sands and the Pavilion, before returning to the Harbour along a different route.

The second starts again at the Harbour and goes west along Marine Parade to the Cliff Lift at the end, where one can take the lift up to the start of the third walk.

The third walk starts at the top end of the Cliff Lift and moves westwards up the Leas as far as the statue of William Harvey.

Acknowledgements

I am most grateful for the advice and suggestions of Paul Harris and Melita Godden on Folkestone history, and Alan Taylor on local fishing. I am also grateful to John Powell, of Marrin's Antiquarian Bookshop in Folkestone, for his remarkable ability to identify the many classic cars which appear in photographs of fifty years ago.

FOLKESTONE THEN AND NOW
ALL IN COLOUR

CONTENTS

Note: All the modern photographs
were taken by the author between 2005 and 2007.

THE FIRST WALK: FROM THE HARBOUR TO THE PAVILION

We start our first walk from the car park opposite the bottom of the Old High Street. This large open area was originally open water, and part of Folkestone Harbour. A little stream, known as the Pent Stream, flowed along Tontine Street and straight into the Harbour. However, the constant problem with the coast around here has been the depositing of shingle, which led to the harbours silting up for over a thousand years. So Folkestone Harbour was much bigger originally.

Before the Folkestone Improvement Act of 1855, the area of the Harbour car park was covered with buildings. This illustration shows the Pent Stream running beneath the windows of the houses. Nowadays the Pent Stream runs underneath Tontine Street and the car park area until it flows under Chummys seafood kiosk and then emerges in the sea under Gigi's café. Luckily, the Inner and Outer Harbours of Folkestone were dredged and do survive.

Before leaving this area, take a look at Chummy's seafood kiosk, a very modern design completed in about 2002. Below the counter we can admire a mosaic showing shellfish, designed by two local artists and completed in 2004. Keeping Chummy's on your right, walk anti-clockwise round the area until you come to the first archway. Go through the archway, walk up till you have Folkestone Trawlers Ltd on your left, walk round the end of that building and look to your left down the next narrow street, to see what used to be one of Folkestone's most picturesque sights.

3

Above is the narrow street, as it appeared in 2006. On the left is Folkestone Trawlers. The building on the far right is a survivor from the 18th century, and possibly the oldest surviving building in the harbour area. It was built as a "smokery", for smoking fish. In 1899 it was taken over by Arthur Goddard, and three generations of Goddards ran it until it closed in 1990. Goddard's name appears over the door in the right hand photo, where we see empty wooden barrels used for salting herrings before they were put in the smokery.

In the middle distance is the archway which forms part of the train viaduct leading down into the harbour station. At present the arch forms an attractive entrance to the old fishing quarter. Most of the railway line is scheduled for demolition, to be replaced by a road. However, one hopes this section can be retained, to continue forming an entrance to this area.

FISHERMANS HOUSES, FOLKESTONE.

In this photo, from about 1905, we see the smokery on the right. To the left of it is a single storey building. This was even earlier, from the 17th century, and was called the Tanlade. Inside it, fishing nets were dipped in a tan-coloured liquid to preserve them. It has now been replaced by the Stade Fish Bar.

To the left of the Tanlade is a tall wooden hut. Such huts, for drying and storing fishing nets, were once a common sight in the South-east, but now survive almost uniquely at Hastings.

At the top of the hut is a beam with a pulley, used for pulling up the nets to their full height. The nets were 18 feet deep, and had to be hung up full length. If the nets were stored in a heap, they would get hot and eventually catch fire. One such net is visible hanging up: they were used for catching sprats, herrings or mackerel. At the time of this photo, the net hut was still in good condition, as we see from the double-flap door on the upper storey, while the ladder below has a handrail fixed on the left-hand side.

5

Fishmarket, Folkestone

A later photograph of some of the old buildings. This time, the Tanlade, on the right of the photo, has a bearded fisherman sitting in front of the open window. He is repairing a fishing net, with a couple of his fellow fishermen gossiping behind him.

But in this photograph, one can see that the tall wooden fishing hut was by now in a very poor state of repair. Comparing with the old photo on the previous page, look at the upper open door. The earlier photo shows two half-door flaps in good condition. By the time of this photo, the lower flap has fallen off, and the upper one shows a primitive patch repair. Even the boards above the door itself are starting to fall off, while the stepladder below has lost its handrail.

Here an anonymous contemporary artist succeeds in making the buildings look even more picturesque, as well as dilapidated, in a painting later reproduced as a postcard. It was this general state of disrepair which eventually led to most of these buildings being demolished and replaced by modern buildings in the late 1930s. They might have needed a lot of repairs to conserve them, but it is only now that we realise how much we lost, by what seemed at the time a straightforward demolition of dilapidated properties.

To continue the walk, move back to stand on the edge of the harbour. You are now looking at the Outer Basin of the Harbour.

The Fishmarket FOLKESTONE

The Outer Basin gets its name because the railway viaduct in the distance divided the harbour in two, creating the Inner Basin on the other side. The railway came to Folkestone in 1843, and the viaduct across the Harbour was completed shortly after.

Above is the completed Burstin Hotel in 2005, looking across the Harbour at high tide. The railway viaduct is one of the steepest in this country: at 1 in 25, it sometimes required no less than five steam engines to haul the carriages up to the junction with the main line.

In 2007 the line was still being used by the Orient-Express line, to offer passengers a return steam trip from London to Folkestone. As an alternative, it also offered a trip to the Continent via the Channel Tunnel, travelling as far as Paris, Zurich and ultimately Venice. But the service to the Orient finished many years ago.

This unusual view shows the Burstin Hotel is its initial form, in about 1980: it is the large white building on the left. It was in fact built in the front garden of the Royal Pavilion Hotel, leaving its predecessor almost untouched: the dark red building on the right in this photo.

During the last War, the Pavilion Hotel was requisitioned by the army, who finally left in 1954. After that it remained empty, till Mr Burstin bought it as flats for the elderly. But once he had built the new modern hotel seen on the left, it must have proved itself much more desirable than its 130-year-old rival. As a result, he demolished most of the rest of the Royal Pavilion Hotel in 1981-2, to extend the Burstin.

In 1988 he sold it, and various companies have owned it since then. During the summer it receives about a thousand visitors a week.

To obtain the next view, continue walking along the side of the harbour away from the viaduct. Turn left after you have passed the Sunny Sands Café, and look back into town.

The above photo was taken during the town's first Harbour Festival of July 2006. That was a one-off event. But from the spring of 2007, there has been a very successful Farmers', Fishing, Art and Craft Market every Sunday beside the Harbour. Known as the Ark Market, it is the biggest of its kind in Kent. It stands on the site of the Ark Café, a listed 17th century building demolished by Mr Jimmy Godden in October 1987.

In the summer, there are occasional jazz concerts opposite the pub called The Mariner. Further down the road lies The Three Mackerel. It was to the Three Mackerel in 1800 that two women smugglers brought in two kegs of spirits, hidden in a laundry basket.

Harbour Point, the houses with green balconies on the far right, was built in about 1992.

The long row of houses seen on the right is part of the 1930s redevelopment of this part of the harbour, though the photo above dates probably from the 1960s. However, walls with large stonework surviving under the arches appear to show that the boat sheds here go back at least a century. They were left as they were, and new houses simply built on top.

In the distance in the photo above, the small white shop offers "Crayze Golf", presumably on the flat ground outside. Most of such entertainments were later shifted to the other side of the Burstin Hotel. But Crayze Golf itself now survives beside the East Pavilion in Wear Bay Road.

The white curving arches on the right conceal several lock-up sheds, as well as steps taking one up hill. To the right or east of these steps, the sheds were used for storing fishing gear, while the one on the west was used for boat-building.

11

Turning our back on the last scene, we now encounter the Sunny Sands: Folkestone's best kept secret. I am one of many who thought for years that the beach at Folkestone was very stony. And so it was, west of the Harbour. But stretching to the East, towards the Warren, is a delightful sandy beach which gets the sun until late in the day, and stays sandy no matter how far the tide goes out. Here we see it in the summer of 2006.

The long promenade of arches was completed in 1935, when it was named Coronation Parade. The structure helps to prevent erosion, and indeed several feet of sand have since built up under the arches.

In the distance can be seen a white tower, one of the Martello towers built in Napoleonic times. One of the earliest paintings of this tower is a watercolour made by Turner in about 1830, showing smuggling on the shore.

This view of about 1960 changed considerably once the enormous concrete structure was built along the back of the beach, with a café on top. This is actually a pumping station for Southern Water, constructed in 2000. Thank goodness its construction has not affected the delights of the beach. Instead, in summer it provides a cafeteria with a splendid view, as well as toilets.

Remarkably, in 2004 Folkestone acquired a second sandy beach further west, under the Leas Cliff Hall. This was when reinforcement to the shoreline, to prevent erosion, resulted in a new beach, replacing the shingle which was there before.

If one now walks down to the sands and stands under one of the arches near the ramp, we see our next view.

Above we see the Sunny Sands, taken in 2006, looking though one of the archways of Coronation Parade. Note the presence of sunshades, now we are conscious of the danger of skin cancer from too much sun on unprotected skin. But in the 1950s there were fewer such worries, though some visitors to the beach stayed fully clothed.

After comparing with the view opposite, the reader has a choice. They may turn back to explore more of interest in central Folkestone. Alternatively, they can walk along the Promenade above the arches to the end, and then take the steps leading to the pathway which winds up towards the Pavilion. Halfway up, the rockery beside the stream used to be a flower garden full of colour. Perhaps one day it will flower again.

Even in the late 1950s, the Sunny Sands were a draw for those who wanted to avoid walking on the shingle of the beach west of the pier. Here we see several bright 1950s dresses, whose owners look on, while their young children amuse themselves with bucket and spade.

In the distance are two boats drawn up beside the Pier. The cranes rising above them were used not just for freight, but also to lift cars onto the boats, using nets and chains.

The ferry service from Folkestone to Boulogne was very important from its start in 1843. It only finished in the year 2000.

At least, when one gets up to the green in front of The Pavilion, we do normally find a flowery display, from which one gets an attractive view of the Harbour, with the big white Burstin Hotel in the distance.

The photo above is from 2005. Just visible in the distance is the spire of the fishermen's church, the second church built in Folkestone. It is called, logically, St. Peter's, after the patron saint of fishermen. We shall be walking past it shortly.

The story goes that originally all the inhabitants of Folkestone went to the ancient parish church of St Mary and St Eanswythe in Folkestone centre. This meant that, understandably, there was a strong fishy smell every Sunday when the fisherfolk joined the great and the good. Lord Radnor then thought of giving the fisherfolk a church of their very own, much closer to the harbour. He duly gave them St. Peter's, in 1862, and the nostrils of the congregation at St. Mary's were duly assuaged. As for the truth of the story, I could not possibly comment.

This photo is from about 1960, with the original Royal Pavilion Hotel visible in the distance, now replaced by the Burstin. Prominent on the left in this photo is a Ford Zephyr or Zodiac Mark II; behind it is a green Austin A35 van. The white car further away is a Zephyr or Zodiac Mark III, with a light blue MG ZB Magnette beyond it.

At this point one could stop at the Pavilion for refreshments and to admire the view. After that, follow the road in front of you - Wear Bay Road –

up and then down the slope, then turn left down the attractive road called The Durlocks. This takes you past the large red building called St Andrews. This used to be a nunnery, and later became a convalescent home. It is now private flats. The fisherman's church is on the next corner.

To start the next walk, continue downhill to the end of The Durlocks, turn right through the archway and you find yourself back in the open area near the harbour.

SECOND WALK: FROM THE HARBOUR TO THE LIFT

This scene can introduce our next walk, which will take us around the harbour. Start in front of the entrance to the Burstin Hotel and look across the harbour at the view. Once again the white Martello tower is visible on the hillside. 74 Martello Towers were built for protection around the SE coast in 1805-8, when invasion by Napoleon was threatened. This Tower is No.3. The photo was taken on 16th June 2007, when the Golden Arrow returned to Folkestone Harbour Station for the last time. At low tide, Folkestone Harbour dries out completely, on both sides of the railway viaduct. This severely restricts water transport, the more so as boats cannot get under the arches at high tide either. There are plans to demolish this viaduct, and if the harbour becomes a marina, as it surely should, we can expect some kind of sill to be built, which will stop the harbour drying out at low tide, but still allow access for the boats.

A photograph taken from high up in the Royal Pavilion Hotel, now replaced by the Burstin. The green Austin A35 van at bottom left indicates a date in the 1950s for this photo. On the right is a coach with the distinctive livery of East Kent buses. This was a Dennis Lancet LV2, which was one of thirty delivered to East Kent in 1954.

Folkestone is remarkable for still having its four Martello Towers, three of them on the East Cliff. Back in the 1960s, Martello Tower No 3 still had its grey colour, like most of the others.

On one occasion in the early 1900s, the family who lived in the tower fired three shots from the cannon, which was still there, to celebrate a family wedding. This caused quite a scare, as the locals thought the French must be shelling the town!

In the far distance are the cliffs near Dover: in front of them now is a new piece of land called Samphire Hoe, created from the spoil produced when digging the Channel Tunnel.

Leaving the entrance of the Burstin, turn right and stop as you reach the corner of the harbour. Looking across it, the scene is still very recognisable.

The building at left on the top of the hill, is no 1 Bayle Parade, over-looking the harbour. This remarkable structure, with a cupola on the top, was built in 1894. Most of the houses in Bayle Parade have elaborate stucco mouldings along their upper pediments. There is a fine German stucco eagle on the end of no 1 - the eagle of Kaiser Wilhelm.

Nowadays obscured by trees in summer, this eagle was added, it is said, when the building was used as the German trade legation, before the First World War.

Another story recounts how during that War, someone was caught signalling towards France. He was court-martialled, sentenced to death and executed in the garden of the house! Between the First and Second World Wars, the house became a Hotel, and was renamed Shangri-La. It is now a private house.

On the far left of the photo above, probably taken in the 1960s, the dark red building is the Royal Pavilion Hotel, of which we see one corner (now replaced by the Burstin Hotel). Beyond it, the grey roofed building was at one time a skating rink – a sport which has suddenly become very popular again. The building was later used as a garage, but now a car park stands on the site. In fact, temporary skating rinks were constructed at Christmas 2005 and in spring 2007 in the harbour area, to give some flavour of possible developments in the future.

Next to the skating rink we see a large white building standing proudly left of centre. This tavern, now called Gillespie's, was for a long time called the London and Paris, as a reminder of the ferry connection which linked Folkestone Harbour to Boulogne.

Nowadays there are still many boats kept in the Harbour, but the Folkestone fishing industry has almost disappeared. Boats originating from Folkestone can be spotted by the initials FE followed by a number.

From almost the same viewpoint, we see here the Royal Pavilion Hotel in more detail, in about 1900. It got its name because of a curious incident in 1843. Back then, the young Queen Victoria was travelling to the continent from Dover. The railway had only been completed from London as far as Folkestone, after which one had to go by road. But the weather was so terrible on this date, there was no way a carriage could reach Dover, for the Queen to stay there. Folkestone was therefore scoured by the courtiers, who reported back that there was absolutely no hotel good enough for the royal party. The solution was for the Queen to be accommodated overnight in a large pavilion built on the beach beside the harbour. A year later, the new hotel got its name from the Queen's pavilion.

The harbour again, perhaps in the 1930s, looking much more romantic in the evening light. The Royal Pavilion Hotel, on the left, was built in the 1840s by the South-Eastern Railway. They had already bought the harbour, and wanted to ensure luxurious accommodation for their passengers travelling to the Continent. The architect for the Hotel was William Cubitt, the same man who designed the viaduct which now carries the railway-line through the back of Folkestone and on to Dover.

If you look to your left at this point, you will be looking down Marine Parade. As you start to walk along it, notice on the right how part of the old Royal Pavilion Hotel has survived, almost hidden behind the Burstin Hotel. Along this part of the walk, the boundary wall on the right still has its gentle white curves, though sadly in need of refurbishment. On the corner stands Pavilion Court, built as a hotel in the 1950s, and now private studio apartments. If you turn right and walk a short distance down Marine Terrace, you see on the right the terracotta mouldings giving the name of the Royal Pavilion Hotel, on the end of the surviving block. You should now return to Marine Parade, and continue walking down it.

The crowds seen on the left (in 2005) are walking from the Sunday market, a market for bargain goods. This was located much further down on the left, next to an amusement park, on the site of the Victorian bandstand. It has now (2007) moved to the centre of town.

Folkestone sea front in about 1910 was clearly an elegant place to stroll or cycle along. In the foreground on the left were well-kept gardens. Further along, the pink building was a very grand crescent, Marine Crescent, now listed Grade II. It was in a very sad state for over a decade, but the former owner, Mr Jimmy Godden, sold it in 2004 to a developer who is restoring it to make luxury apartments, all under the supervision of English Heritage and local architects Roger Joyce Associates.

This is what should happen to other such neglected buildings.

In the distance, one can just see a bandstand with a large audience gathered around. The amusement park which replaced the bandstand and gardens has now gone also, and there are exciting plans for the redevelopment of the whole of this area. Folkestone still has a bandstand with regular summer concerts, but it is above the cliff, on the Leas.

Walking past Marine Crescent, we come to the Cliff Lift, of which Folkestone has been proud ever since its completion in 1885. It is one of only three such lifts surviving in Britain, unusual because it is hydraulic, in other words, powered by water. The hydraulic lift which survives in Saltburn, Yorkshire, was built a year earlier, in 1884, and had stained glass windows added to it in 1991.

In Folkestone, there are water tanks at top and bottom of the lift: indeed, they explain the presence of the ugly red and white bollards, which are to protect the lower tanks from vehicles driving over them and weakening their covering. These will be removed when or if lottery funding is found for restoration work. One of Folkestone's best known historians, Eamonn Rooney, is often found operating the lift from this lower station.

The Cliff Railway Folkestone.

The view above is postmarked 1909. The principal difference is that the lifts seen on the right, with their sloping roofs and stepped interiors, are no longer visible. They were part of a second lift, introduced later, which closed in the 1980s. However, one such stepped carriage does survive elsewhere, awaiting refurbishment.

Both photos are somewhat prosaic presentations of the lift. This lack of interest must have inspired one early photographer to go back on a busy sunny day to photograph the scene again. On sunny days, people visited the pier, which was just opposite the lift, so a much busier scene could be captured.

THE LIFT - FOLKESTONE

The photographer of the picture above visited the cliff lift in around 1923 (the date this card was posted). It was sunny, and lots of people were around. Indeed, the two men in boaters in the middle have clearly just been swimming, as one has his towel rolled up under his arm. The trouble is, the presence of visitors also attracts caterers selling refreshments. So there was a great big Lyons lorry selling tea, coffee and cocoa, parked right in front of the cliff lift building. If the photographer had waited till the lorry left, all the people would have gone too. So this was the best photo he could manage, and the company now started selling a card, showing this busy summer scene.

Back at base, however, probably in Germany, where many such cards were originally produced, one of those in charge must have thought it ridiculous to show a great big lorry blocking the view of this tourist attraction. They could not afford to send the photographer all the way back to take another shot. So instead they decided to "touch up" his photo.

They obliterated the image of the lorry, and then painted in the window to mirror the one they could see on the left. What they didn't know was that the central portico has a smaller portico on either side, so they failed to paint in the portico on the right. (I reproduce the lower half of the picture, where the doctoring has gone on.) Retouching of photographs goes back more than a century!

34967. FOLKESTONE: PIER FROM LEAS.

Almost opposite the Cliff Lift used to stand Folkestone Pier, known as the Victoria Pier. Both these views date from about 1905. Above, elegant octagonal kiosks flank the entrance, while the lawns on either side support white tables and chairs all ready for tea. In 1910 a skating rink was added on the west (right) side of the pier.

The pavilion theatre at the far end could seat up to 1000, and entertainers like Marie Lloyd appeared there. In 1906 it was announced that Lillie Langtry (mistress of Edward VII), was going to appear, and ticket prices were high. But she only appeared for 20 minutes, in a very short play. When the audience realised she was not going to reappear, they started booing and asking for their money back. Eventually three policemen had to be called to clear the theatre!

FOLKESTONE PIER.

The pier was completed in 1888, and was nearly 700 feet long and 30 feet wide. The ornamental garden on the east (left) side was lit up at night, and concerts occasionally given there. Sadly, the theatre at the end burnt down in 1945, and the rest of the pier was taken down in 1954. Up till 2002, one could still see the outline of the base of the entrance kiosks in the concrete. Now, the only visible trace of the pier is the remains of one iron bracket.

The picture above is actually what was called an Oilette, quite a skilled oil-painting of the Pier, reproduced as a postcard. The entrance buildings of the Cliff Lift are visible at the bottom of this photo.

The Beach, Folkestone.

This view was actually taken from Folkestone Pier, looking out from the Theatre at the end. In contrast to the largely empty scene often seen now, this is how it sometimes looked 100 years ago: filled with spectators. This photo must have been taken during the Folkestone Regatta: hence the rowing boats visible on the beach and at sea. Large crowds like this could still be seen when the Folkestone Air Show took place in the 1990s. The dark red building with an arched entrance in the right foreground was the lifeboat house.

The picture above shows two sorts of bathing carriages on the beach. At left are the horse-drawn carriages, which allowed people to undress in comparative privacy before getting into the water. These were to be seen at almost all resorts in Edwardian times. But at the extreme right are two patent carriages invented by a Mr Fagg (an ancient Kentish surname), and in use at Folkestone. These were almost like railway carriages, which ran on rails down into the water. In the foreground is one of the two pleasure boats, which sailed along the beach. This one has survived and is now in the Isles of Scilly.

THIRD WALK: ALONG THE LEAS,
FROM THE LIFT TO THE HARVEY STATUE

Take the cliff lift to the top, which is known as the Leas, and walk down the slope a short distance. Nowadays we just see a vast concrete area below. But looking down in about 1960 you would have seen the view above. The swimming pool was a major attraction of the beach at this point, along with the boating pool just visible beyond it. One can tell how popular they were, by the fact that in this picture they are being well used, and numerous cars are parked nearby.

Above is a close-up view of the busy swimming pool on a sunny day in about 1956, with giant red and yellow rubber rings in use. There are lots of divers waiting to use the four diving boards, and a notice that the deep end was nine foot deep. The pool was kept at a constant 70°. Note two large red double-decker buses in the distance. Had they brought visitors all the way down from London?

The swimming pool was built in 1936 and lasted till 1981, when the whole area was bought by Mr Jimmy Godden. Within two years he had closed and filled in both swimming and boating pools.

On the left can be seen Marine Terrace, already looking distinctly shabby in the 1950s. In 2007, renovation on the terrace was largely complete.

Turn back now to look uphill at the road known as the Lower Leas. The tall high-rise on the far right is No 1 The Leas. This was built as offices in the 1970s, one of its occupants being the Welfare Insurance Company, which later moved to Exeter. It has now become entirely private apartments.

This block and the flats beyond it replaced the Bristol Hotel, which claimed it was "the first hotel on the Leas", and the Wythenshawe Hotel, which boasted "Interspring Beds, Electric Fires and Boiling Rings"!

THE LOWER LEAS, FOLKESTONE.

The postcard view above was posted in 1955, but the photo may well date from the 1930s. Above the lift on the left are notices reading, "The Lift: Shortest Way to Bathing Pool." Presumably the owners of the pool were anxious to encourage its use. On the right, a line of cars, several of which appear to date from the thirties. The white van advertises, "Spencers: Makers of Gymnastic Equipment since 1779."

Note one car in the distance, coming towards us: so the road along the Leas was not yet one-way.

The lady who wrote on this card in 1955 said, "I think you would like Folkestone. The trippers stay at the bottom near the harbour, and on the Leas there are no crowds and no litter. There is always a cool breeze too."

The flats on the far right are called Priors Leas, replacing a former house with the same name. The further group of flats, in the middle of the photo, is called White Cliffs, appropriately, since that in fact is what the buildings look like.

The gap between the two blocks of flats marks what is now the Leas Club. This attractive building, with much terracotta decoration facing the road, was known as The Leas Pavilion Tea Rooms when it opened in 1902. As the two tall buildings either side claimed the right of Ancient Lights, the tea rooms had to be built beneath ground level so as not to obstruct the daylight either side. In 1928, a stage was built inside, and tea matinees started, presenting professional theatre. The trouble was, tea continued to be served while the performances went on, so serious moments in a play could be interrupted by the clatter of teacups and "More tea, vicar?" In 1929 the Arthur Brough Players moved in (Peter Barkworth was part of the company in the 1950s), and the theatre lasted till 1984.

The view above is from 1970, when they were just completing the building of Priors Leas. In the photo, the notice next to the Lift read, "Lift to Beach, Bathing Pool, Amusements, Harbour and Coach Park." During dry weather, the outline of the lift's upper water-tanks can be seen in the grass beside the lift.

The elegant building with the green shades and balconies was the Longford Hotel, at no 7 The Leas. This belonged to the Folkestone Estate and was demolished, soon after a serious fire in about 1990. By 1970 hotels in Folkestone were becoming less popular. People could now afford to take their holidays abroad, so flats were regarded as more lucrative.

Several cars are visible on the right of the photo above. They are, from right to left, a white Hillman Avenger, green Vauxhall FB Viva, red Austin or Morris 1100, and lastly a Mini.

We have now moved substantially up the slope, and have come to the flowerbeds just before we reach the Leas Cliff Hall. The first major building on the left is now the Southcliffe Hotel, which caters for a large number of coach parties. This is something which Saga Holidays did when it was starting in the 1950s. They brought people down from northern England to stay at the Rhodesia Hotel, and have a week enjoying the sunshine of the SE coast. There is a bar called The Office next to the Southcliffe. George Cooper House has been added on the end, while on the next corner is the Carlton Hotel.

The view above was taken, in about 1959, from the roof of the Leas Cliff Hall, which is no longer accessible. People emerging up the hidden stairs on the right will have parked their cars below. The meticulous flowerbeds are still there, though with a simpler layout. This card is said to date from 1959: one wonders if this is shown by the crane visible in the far distance: perhaps this was being used to work on the Cliff Lift.

The first parked car is a Vauxhall, with an Austin A560 behind it, while the car passing them is a Humber Hawk. Further along, the yellow car is an Austin A40, with a Ford Prefect behind it.

The modern view from the Clifton Hotel, looking down on the statue of William Harvey.

The large building on the right, with the green roof, is the Leas Cliff Hall. The Hall was opened in 1927, and is still Folkestone's primary place of entertainment. One striking change between the two photographs is the substantial rebuilding of the Leas Cliff Hall in 1982. This provided for the addition of a substantial foyer next to the booking office, which is used in the daytime as a café. A large chessboard pattern was also added to the roof of the terrace above the Hall. Sadly, no-one seems to use it for outdoor chess. Further improvements to the Hall were made in 2005, when a lift was added to allow easier transport for disabled people down to the lower storeys and conference hall.

This photo was taken from a lower floor of the Clifton Hotel in about1970, and gives us a view of the Leas Cliff Hall before the 1982 improvements.

Two points to note. Half hidden by the statue one can see a lady being pushed in a wheelchair. In those days, before kerbs were specially lowered, the simplest way to navigate a wheelchair was to push it along the gutter! Another curiosity is the figures of the two young men in black, one of whom is pushing a bicycle. Both appear to be wearing a half-length academic black gown as used by undergraduates. Now where would they be from?

Meantime, we may note a white car with a red roof about to turn the corner. It is a Sunbeam Rapier, complete with its distinctive tailfins. At far right, the parked grey car is a Morris Minor, and behind it is a white Austin or Morris 1800. The blue car with a white roof is a Hillman Minx. The big red lorry is a BMC FG van. It has Cadburys inscribed on it, and in front of it is a white Vauxhall Victor FC101.

The statue to William Harvey (1578-1657) dominates the scene at this point. He was born and raised in Folkestone, where his father was Mayor. Harvey was the man who discovered the circulation of the blood, and the 3rd of June 2007 marked the 350th anniversary of his death. There is an annual ceremony here in June to commemorate him. The statue was put up in 1881, sculpted by Albert Joy. A similar one stands near the entrance to the William Harvey Hospital in Ashford.

However, the Langhorne Hotel visible in the earlier photograph has disappeared – or rather, the block at the end. The name has been taken by the Langhorne Garden Hotel, at the other end of the block. Nowadays, the clean lines of the attractive art-deco-type Skuba Bar looks out towards the Leas Cliff Hall.

Apparently, the Langhorne Hotel fell down, with a great crash, in 1947. There had been extensive shelling of Folkestone during the Second World War, and this caused considerable vibration, as well as destruction, in the area. The Hotel was, sadly, just one more casualty of the War, but fell two years after it.

22402   Folkestone.   Harvey Statue.

This view shows the scene in about 1905. Notice the young lad wearing a sailor suit. This had nothing to do with the Navy – it was just fashionable clothing for young boys in Edwardian times.

At the far end of the block on the right, away from the viewer, now stands the Langhorne Garden Hotel, facing Sandgate Road. It was to this hotel, then called The Norfolk, that William Morris, the Victorian painter, craftsman and campaigner, came to recuperate in June 1896. One of the famous Pre-Raphaelite artists, he was only 62 but was already seriously ill with tuberculosis. He was hoping the sea air of Folkestone would do him good, and enjoyed his three weeks here.

He wrote, "Every morning we drive down to the harbour (it is to far for me to walk there), and then I toddle about, and sit down, lean over the chains, and rather enjoy it, especially if there are any craft about." He died back in Hammersmith later that year.

The biggest change in the scene is that the extensive gardens which lay next door to the Langhorne Hotel (now the Skuba Bar) have now been replaced by the block of flats called Carlton Leas. These flats, and the gardens that preceded them, were all built on top of the underground car park which serves the Leas. The entrance to the car park, in Sandgate Road, used to be a simple low entrance. But now that end as well has a block of flats above it, called The Waldorf Apartments, built in 2005.

In the distance on the left the white building is the Southcliffe Hotel, barely visible in the modern photo, where Carlton Leas block the view.

At bottom left is a white car, actually an Austin A60. Before they had invented cardboard windscreen protectors, the only way to keep out the scorching heat of the sun was to use a tartan rug, as the owners have done here.

The parked cars ranged along the road start with a grey Austin A55 at bottom right. The off-white car with a black roof is a Riley 4/72, while the red car with a white roof is a Ford Cortina Mark I Estate.

On this day in 1970, there was a magnificent view down to the Harbour and Pier in the distance, looking in fact along most of the distance we have covered in these three walks.

Nicholas Reed

Nicholas Reed grew up in Dulwich, London. He studied classics and Roman archaeology at Oxford and elsewhere, and took part in some thirty archaeological excavations. While in SE London in the 1980s, he became Founder-Chairman of the Friends of Shakespeare's Globe and of the Friends of West Norwood Cemetery. In the 1990s he was Founder-Chairman of the Edith Nesbit Society, and also edited the Newsletters of the Norwood Society and the Dulwich Society. His book *Camille Pissarro at Crystal Palace* has been reprinted twice since 1987, while his book *Crystal Palace and the Norwoods* was published by Chalford Publishing in 1995.

Since 1984 he has specialised in art history, and he became a NADFAS lecturer in 1991. He has written five books on the Impressionists in England, and another on Frost Fairs on the Frozen Thames. During the 1990s, through his publishing arm Lilburne Press, he published five biographies of writers, and from 2001 to 2007 he was Chairman of the Alliance of Literary Societies.

Nicholas moved to Folkestone in 2003, when he started to publish books on the locality. He has also been active in the pressure group *Go Folkestone*.

Lilburne Press

Lilburne Press published Nicholas's *Smuggling in Folkestone* in 2005, and has been publishing the monthly magazine *Folkestone Creative* since July of that year.

Earlier in 2007 Lilburne Press published a book on William Harvey, by Paul Harris, while this is Nicholas's second local history book on the Folkestone area. For a full list of books from Lilburne Press, see www.lilburnepress.co.uk.

48